PATHFINDER EDITION

By Zahi Hawass

CONTENTS


2 King Tut

8 Rooms in a Tomb

10 Buried Treasures

12 Concept Check

KENNETH GARRETT

**Big Meeting.** *Scientist Zahi Hawass looks at King Tut.*

# King Tut

## Modern science comes face-to-face with an ancient mystery.

By Zahi Hawass
Director of Excavations at the Giza Pyramids and the Valley of the Golden Mummies; and a National Geographic Explorer–in–Residence

## Dates in a Mummy Mystery

**3,327 years ago**
King Tut dies suddenly and is buried.

**83 years ago**
Englishman Howard Carter finds Tut's tomb.

**37 years ago**
X-ray of Tut's head sparks murder theories.

**Present**
Modern medical tools help experts study King Tut's mummy.

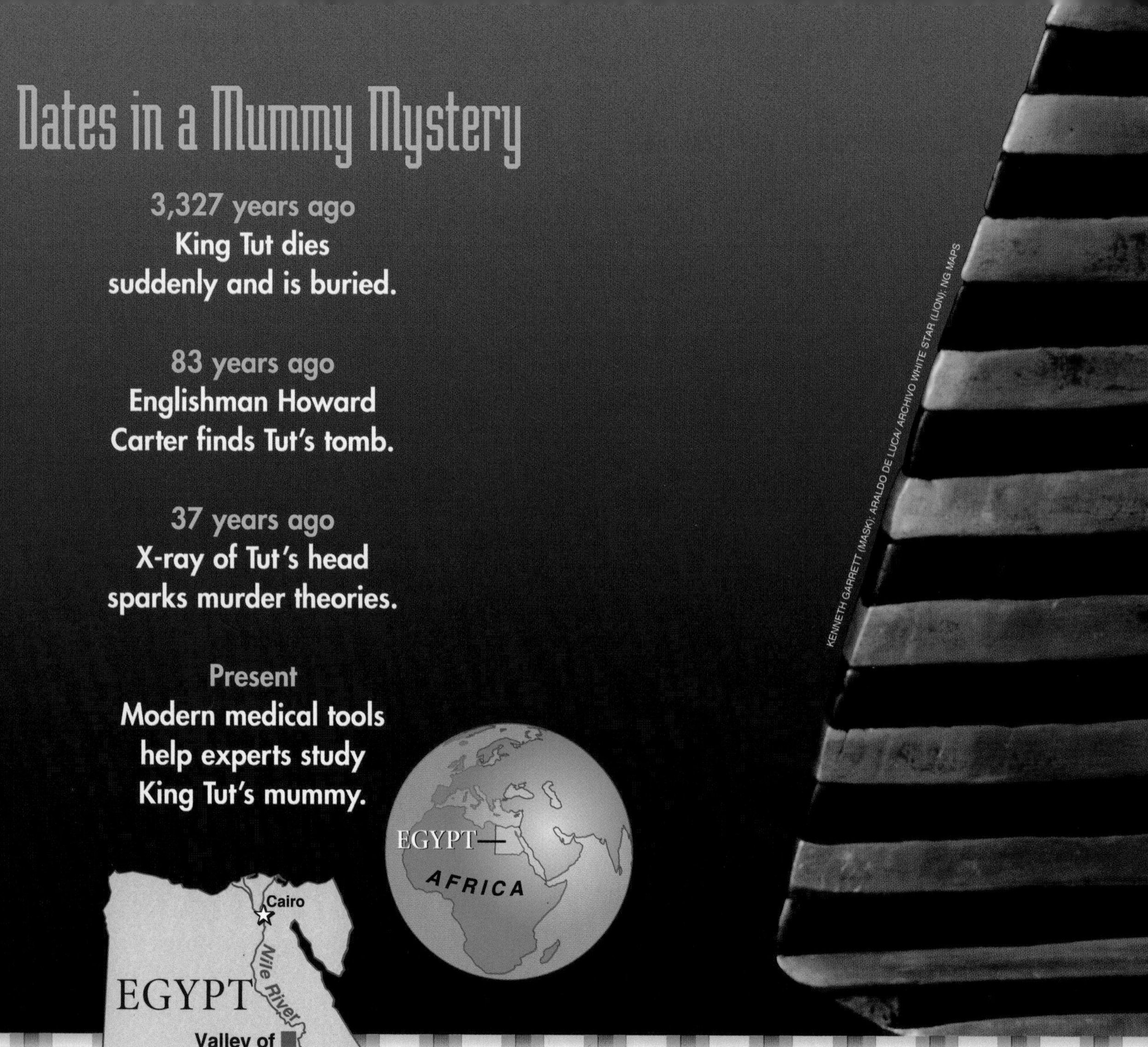


I felt like I was holding my heart in my hands. That's how nervous I was. After all, my team of scientists was taking the world's most famous **mummy** out of its tomb!

If anything went wrong, I'd be in serious trouble. It could even mean the end of my career as an **archaeologist.** That's a scientist who studies the past by looking at what people left behind. My work often involves seeing what items people buried with their dead. Those things help tell us about life in ancient Egypt.

**Famous Face.** *TOP: This world-famous mask shows King Tut in his royal clothing. It was put over the king's face before his coffin was closed.*

## Who Was King Tut?

The tomb that made me so nervous belongs to an Egyptian **pharaoh,** or king. His name was Tutankhamun (too tong KAH mun). You may know him as King Tut.

Tut was born about 3,346 years ago. We don't know exactly who his parents were. At eight or nine, Tut became king. The young pharaoh governed some two million people. Adult officials probably made most decisions, though.

After nine or so years on the throne, Tut suddenly died. He was buried in a treasure-filled tomb. It lies in the Valley of the Kings. The site is near the center of modern Egypt. The valley's rocky walls hide 62 ancient tombs. Many belong to pharaohs.

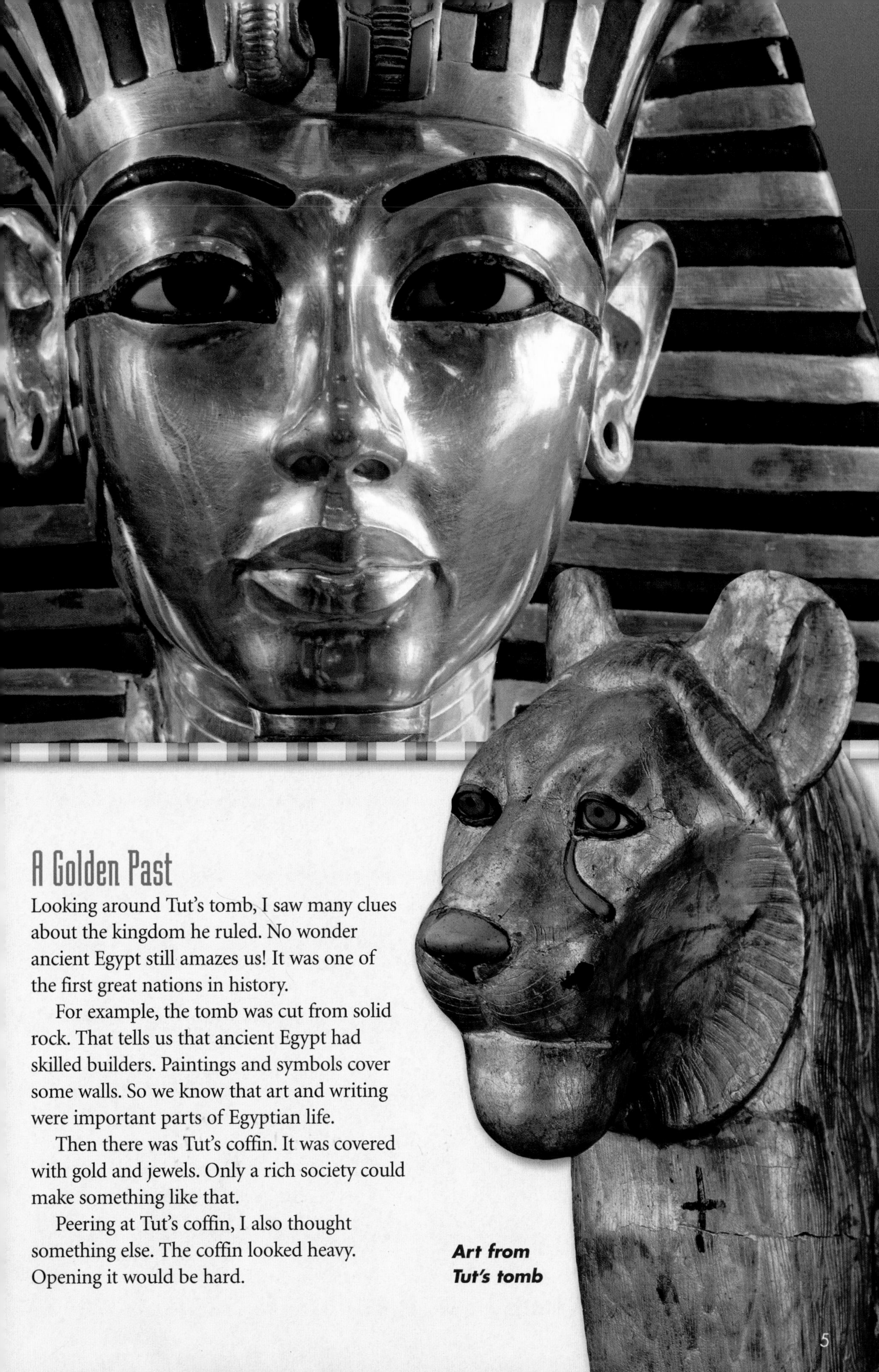

# A Golden Past

Looking around Tut's tomb, I saw many clues about the kingdom he ruled. No wonder ancient Egypt still amazes us! It was one of the first great nations in history.

For example, the tomb was cut from solid rock. That tells us that ancient Egypt had skilled builders. Paintings and symbols cover some walls. So we know that art and writing were important parts of Egyptian life.

Then there was Tut's coffin. It was covered with gold and jewels. Only a rich society could make something like that.

Peering at Tut's coffin, I also thought something else. The coffin looked heavy. Opening it would be hard.

***Art from Tut's tomb***

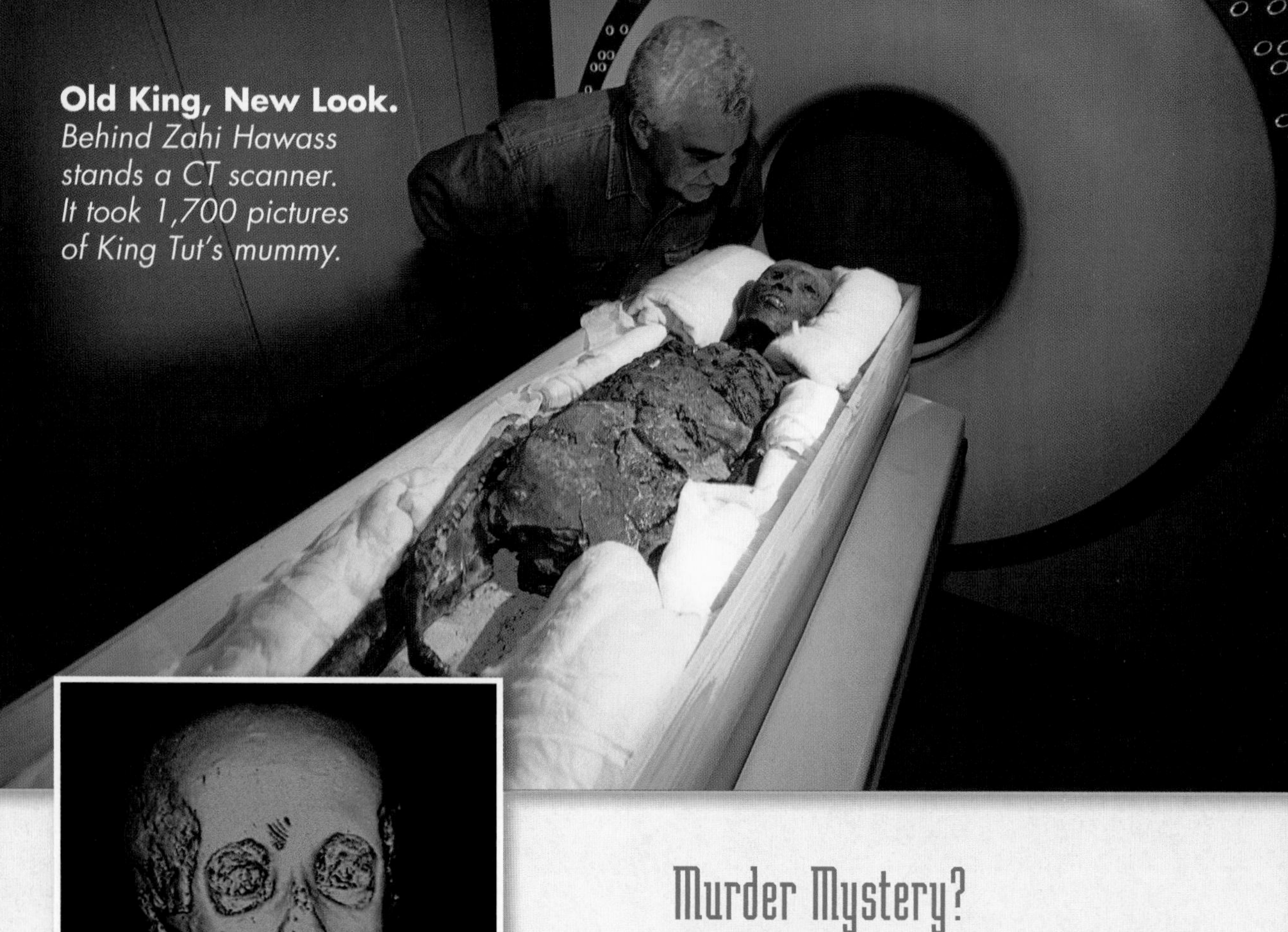

**Old King, New Look.** *Behind Zahi Hawass stands a CT scanner. It took 1,700 pictures of King Tut's mummy.*

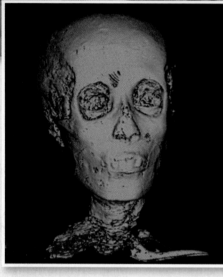

KENNETH GARRETT (BOTH)

**High-Tech History.** *Computers made this image of King Tut's head.*

## Awesome Moment

My team used thick ropes to lift the coffin lid. Workers strained. Ropes groaned. Minutes crawled. The coffin opened.

Then came the moment to meet the king face-to-face. I took the cover from his head. Our faces were just inches apart.

Looking at Tut's young face and his buckteeth, I smiled. Over the years, this young king has made everyone wonder about him.

People have asked many questions about Tut. One stands out. How did the pharaoh die?

## Murder Mystery?

King Tut was 19 when he died. Even for his time, that was young. People have wondered why the king died so young. Was he too weak or sickly to live very long?

Some people raised more dramatic questions. In 1968, an x-ray showed a fuzzy area at the back of Tut's head. Was it an injury? Had someone murdered the king?

I thought modern medical tools might help us solve the mystery. So we placed Tut in a **CT scanner.** It shows what is inside a body.

The scanner took 1,700 pictures of King Tut. My team spent two months studying them. We looked. We thought. We argued.

In the end, we agreed about two big things. First of all, Tut seemed generally healthy. The king had strong bones and good teeth. His body showed no sign of disease.

Second, the mummy also showed no signs of violent death. A blow to the head would have left clear marks. We found none.

Answering old questions, the team found a new one. We saw that Tut's left leg was broken just above the knee. How did that happen? This time, we didn't agree on an answer.

## Fractured Views

Some of us thought Tut broke his leg shortly before dying. The break would likely have torn the skin. Perhaps germs infected the wound. That could have made Tut sick enough to die.

Others disagreed. They said the break happened after Tut died.

If Tut didn't break his leg, who did? Maybe there was an accident while priests prepared the body for burial. The break could also date from the 1920s. That's when scientists first took Tut out of his coffin. To do so, they cut the mummy into pieces.

## Picturing the Past

We may never solve the mystery of King Tut's leg. In time, more scientists will study the images. Experts will have new and different ideas about how he died. As always in Egypt, there is much more to learn.

That learning isn't limited to King Tut. The CT scanner will help us study many other mummies too. We'll look at great kings and humble workers. All those pictures will let us see ancient Egypt in wonderful new ways.

*What do you want to know about Egyptian mummies? What tools could you use to help you find answers to your questions?*

## Wordwise

**archaeologist:** scientist who studies items and places from the past

**CT scanner:** medical tool that shows the insides of a body

**mummy:** body preserved by drying

**pharaoh:** ruler in ancient Egypt

KENNETH GARRETT, ART BY ELISABETH DAYNÈS

## The Face of History

What did King Tut look like? A team of scientists and artists recently tried to find out. They began by studying CT scans. Based on the pictures, the team created a model of Tut's skull.

Team members measured the skull. That helped them figure out the shape of Tut's face. An artist used the data to make the model below.

The artist had to guess at the color of Tut's skin. Modern Egyptians range from very light to quite dark. So the artist picked a shade in the middle.

# Rooms in a Tomb

King Tut's underground tomb had four main rooms. The rooms were packed with items the pharaoh would need in his life after death. This diagram shows what the rooms looked like when they were first discovered.

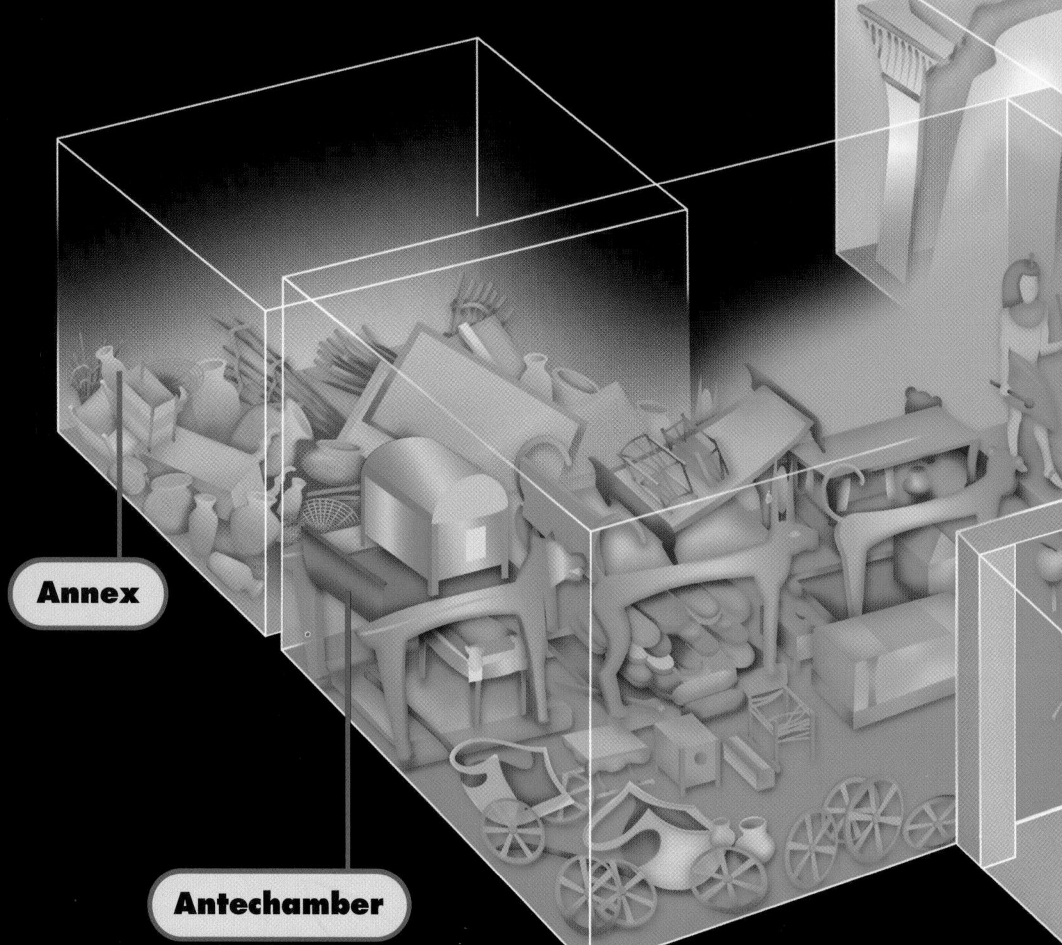


**Annex:** You'll find this small room next to the antechamber. It provided extra storage for items such as chairs, stools, boxes, and baskets.

**Antechamber:** This room connected the entrance passage to the burial chamber. It contained couches, chests, statues, parts of several chariots, a throne, and other supplies.

**Burial chamber:** The sarcophagus holding King Tut's mummy was in this room.

**Treasury:** Look for this room next to the burial chamber. It contained important artifacts. A tall chest held the pharaoh's liver, lungs, stomach, and intestines.

**Entrance passage:** This hallway led to the antechamber.

DAWN RIPPLE MCFADIN

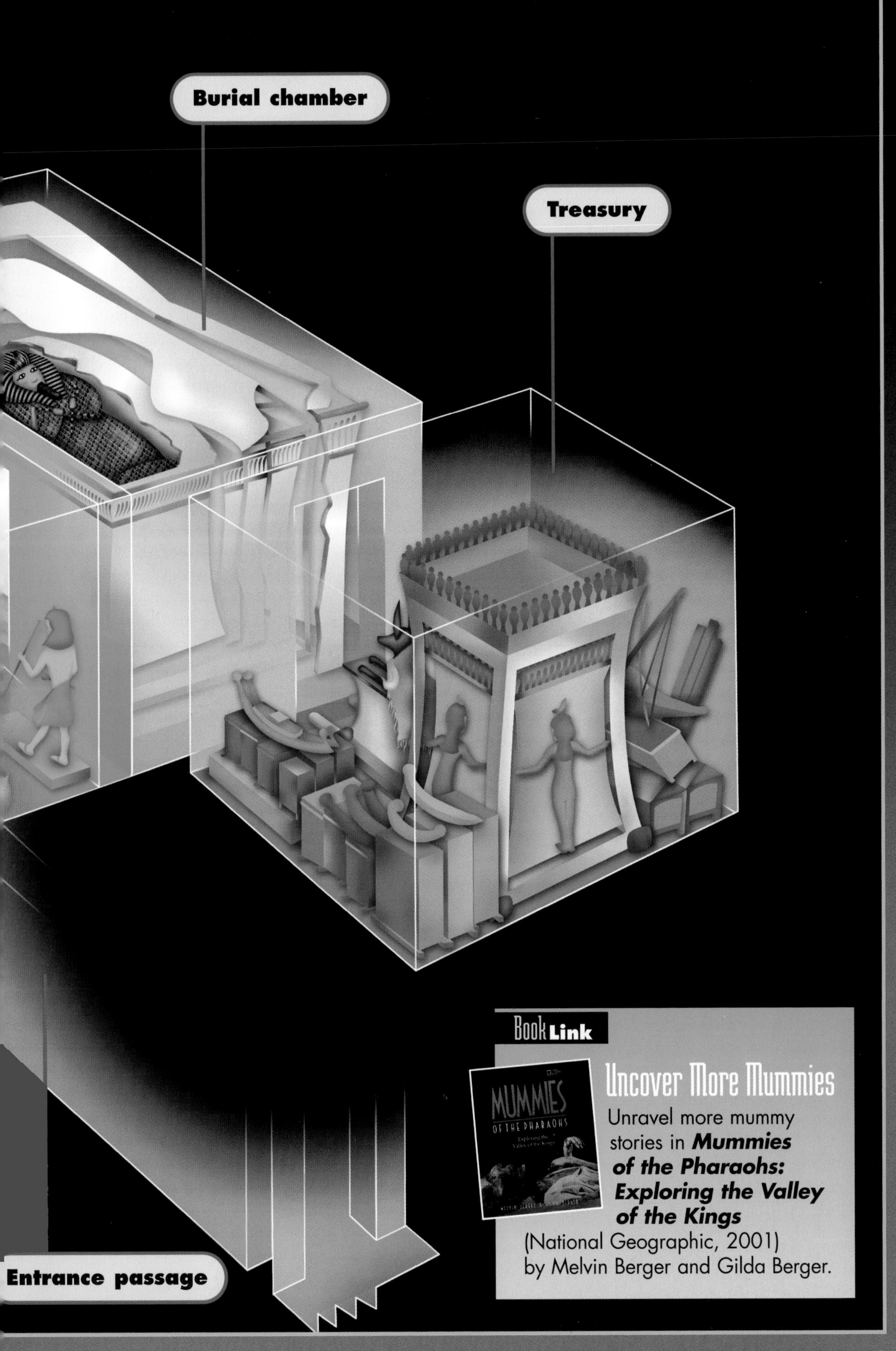


**Book Link**

## Uncover More Mummies

Unravel more mummy stories in ***Mummies of the Pharaohs: Exploring the Valley of the Kings*** (National Geographic, 2001) by Melvin Berger and Gilda Berger.

# Buried Treasures

When archaeologists first explored King Tut's burial chamber, they had no idea what they would find. They had to work through many layers to discover the treasures inside the tomb. Deep inside the layers, they found King Tut's body. A gold mask covered his head and shoulders. Yet even when archaeologists took off the mask, they didn't know all that Tut had to tell them. Today, archaeologists continue to make new discoveries about King Tut with the help of CT scanners and other tools.

ART BY DAMNFX

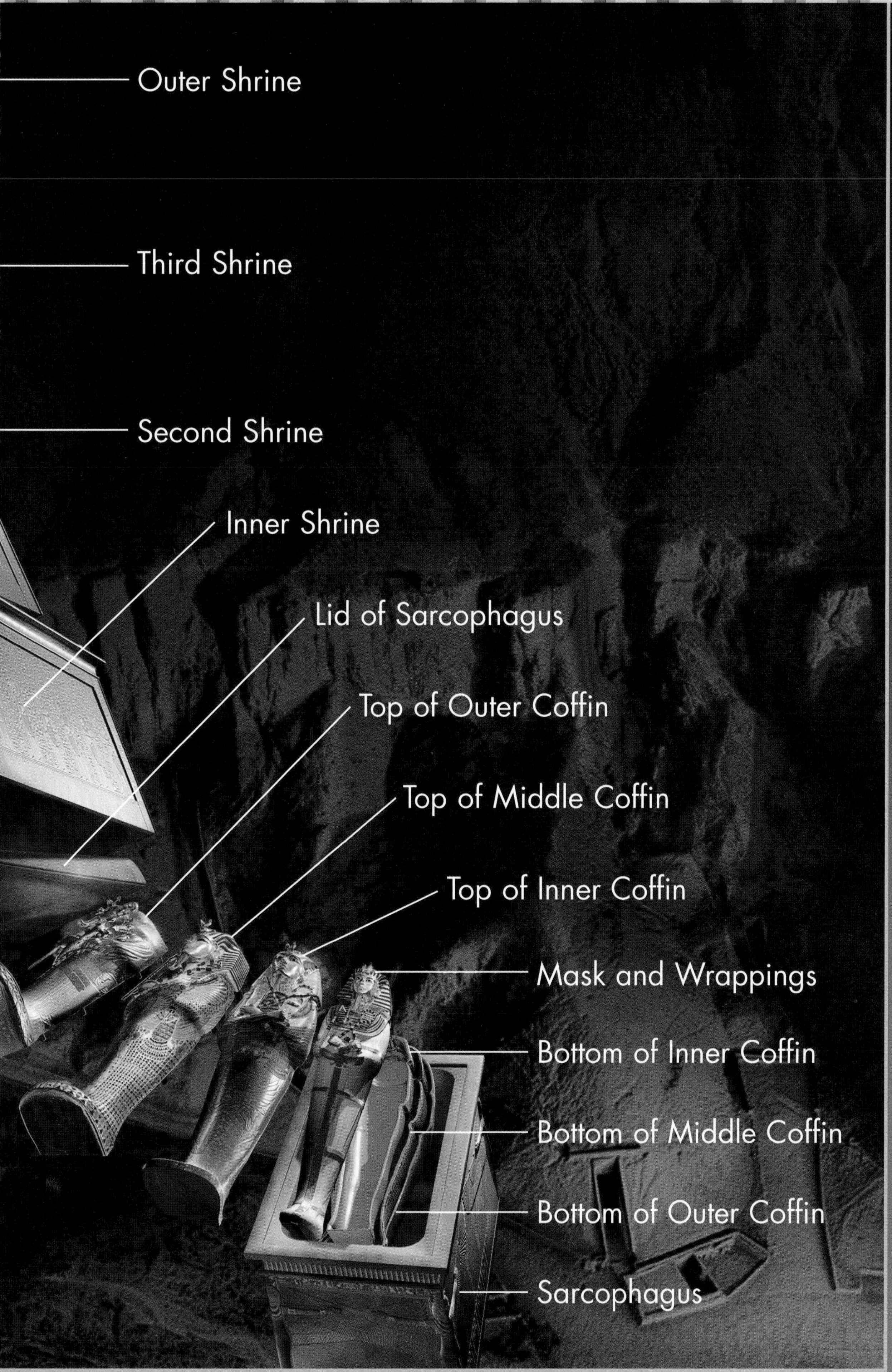

Outer Shrine

Third Shrine

Second Shrine

Inner Shrine

Lid of Sarcophagus

Top of Outer Coffin

Top of Middle Coffin

Top of Inner Coffin

Mask and Wrappings

Bottom of Inner Coffin

Bottom of Middle Coffin

Bottom of Outer Coffin

Sarcophagus

# King Tut

**It's time to uncover what you've learned about King Tut.**

1. Who was King Tut?
2. What did King Tut's tomb tell about ancient Egyptian life?
3. What mysteries did Zahi Hawass try to explain?
4. How did technology help answer Hawass's questions about King Tut?
5. How did King Tut break his leg? Why does it matter?

KENNETH GARRETT